Printed in the United States of America

First Printing, 2017

Published by Songbird Artistry

48 Newgate Road

Pittsburgh, PA 15202

www.songbirdartistry.com

I0489344

You can write to Debbie at debo1960@aol.com

Introduction

This coloring book is dedicated to the memory of my husband, Larry Jacknin. Larry was diagnosed with ALS in September 2013 and stopped working at the beginning of 2014.

Larry and I made a very conscious choice to live life. He had ALS but the disease would not define who he was nor what he could do. While Larry was battling ALS, we traveled to Israel, went to Colorado for his daughter's wedding, wintered in Florida, and enjoyed time with family and friends.

The most important thing we tried to convey is that everyone in life faces challenges. ALS was a tough diagnosis to receive but instead of focusing on the negative, we focused on what Larry could do.

We had always dreamed of being artists, and when Larry left work we spent our spare time turning what we saw and felt into stained-glass mosaics. Larry passed away February 23, 2016. In the two years after he stopped working we created over fifty pieces of art together.

You'll find many of the works that Larry and I created together in the pages of this book, together with some reminisces about the artworks and our life together.

Larry was a man who was bright, imaginative and loving. He listened, cared deeply for his friends and family, and pressed on when others might have given up. It is my hope that in reading this book and coloring in our mosaics that you might feel some of that spirit yourself.

Debbie Maier Jacknin

Pittsburgh, 2017

Tree of Life

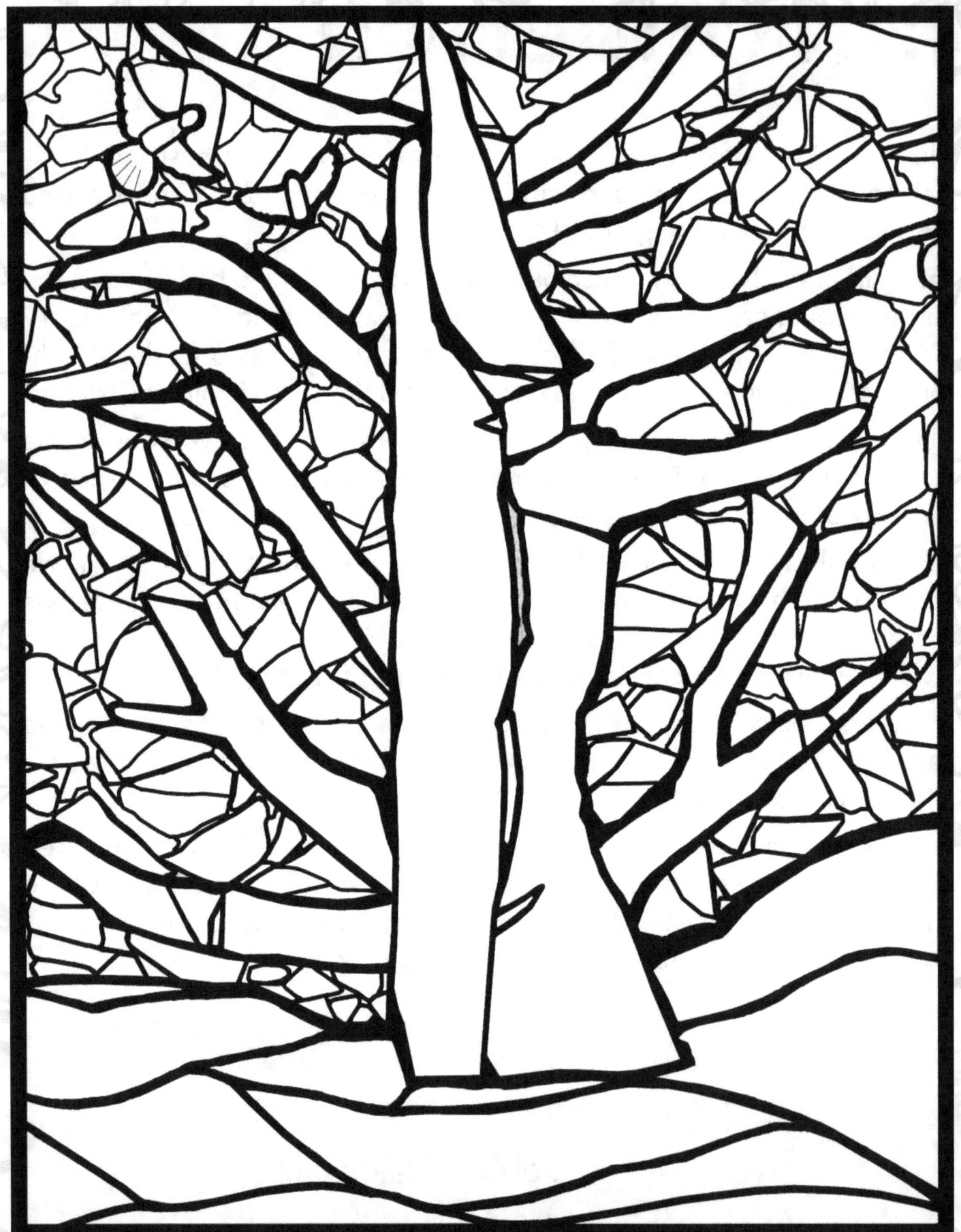

Tree of Life

The Tree of Life stained glass mosaic was inspired by our trip to Israel in February and March 2014. While there, Larry and I went to Tzfat which is located on the top of one of Israel's mountains. To get there, we drove on a twisty, windy road. We were very hungry and ready to get out of the car but the GPS seemed to be taking us in circles.

Finally we stopped and saw a man who was with his young son. We asked if they knew the location of our bed and breakfast. He said yes, but that it was a little hard to find and offered to take us there. We walked up and down steps, around corners and through alleys.

Finally, he pointed to a blue door at the end of another long alley. He asked about our bags and showed us the best place to park but explained that with all the one way circular streets it would be best if he drove with us and he would show us the way. We walked back to our car and when we were almost there someone else asked him for directions and he sent his young son off to help another stranger while he came in our car with us.

He was aware of Larry's disability and offered to carry our bags. When we thanked him, he responded, "no, really, it is my pleasure to help."

A stranger who saw two people in need and helped. Imagine this world if we all thought this way.

We were told Tzfat was a spiritual and magical place - and we agreed. It is said that the first books of Kabbalah were written there. We had the privilege of studying with two artist-teachers, and there learned that Kabbalah teaches a lot about giving and receiving.

Look closely at the Tree of Life mosaic and notice that there are two sides to the trunk. They represent giving and receiving. Larry was always the type of person who liked to help others. Because of his disease, he had to learn to receive help for simple tasks that many of us take for granted. Larry and I found that this brings out the best in others as most people are more than happy to help. This renewed his faith in mankind.

If you look at the trunks of the tree on the original (on the back cover) and you will see a drop of red. This represents our selfish side. The tree shows that you need to be able to give and receive to be in balance. As you go higher on the tree you get closer to God.

Cottage by the Lake

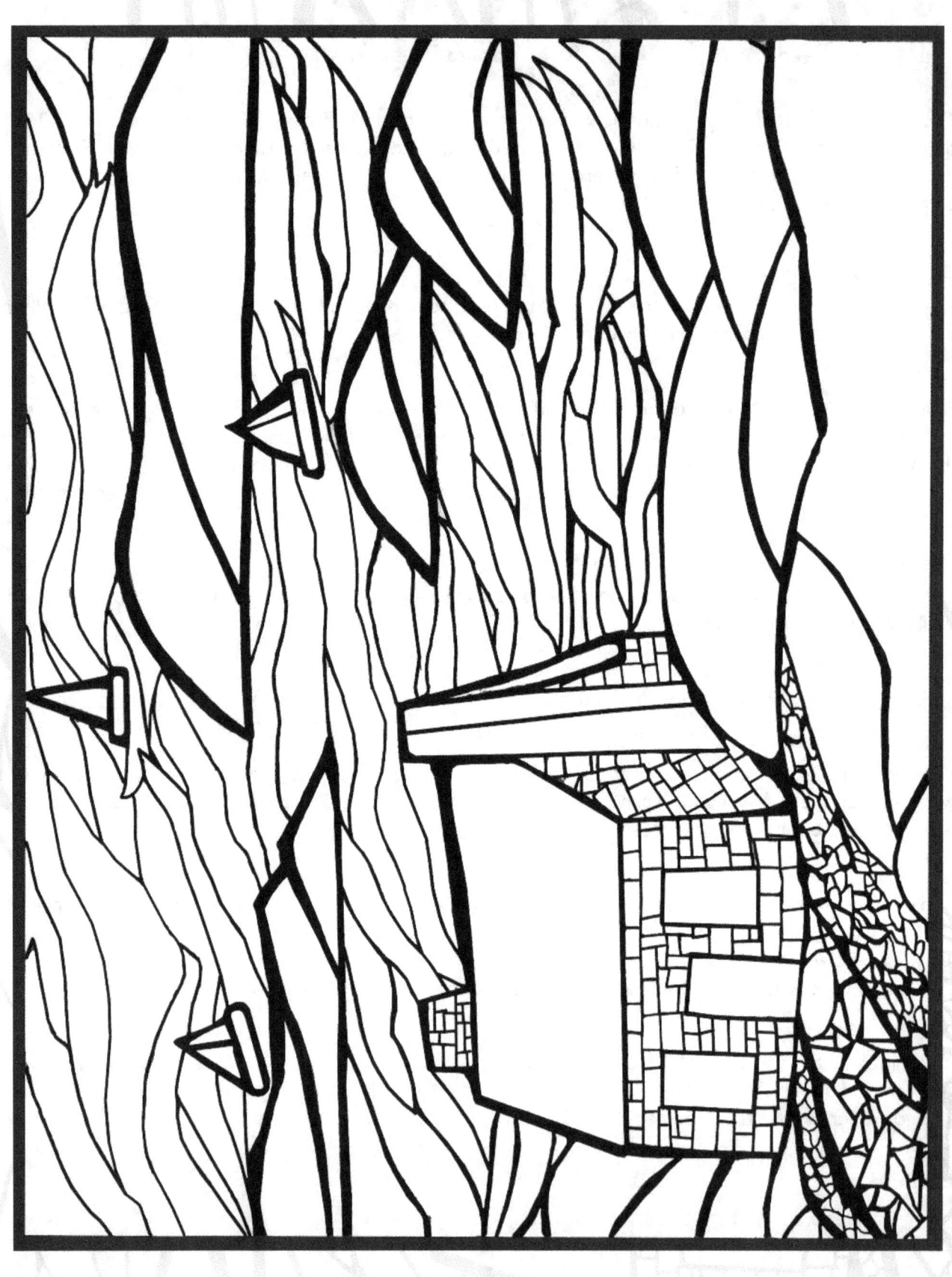

Fall Barn

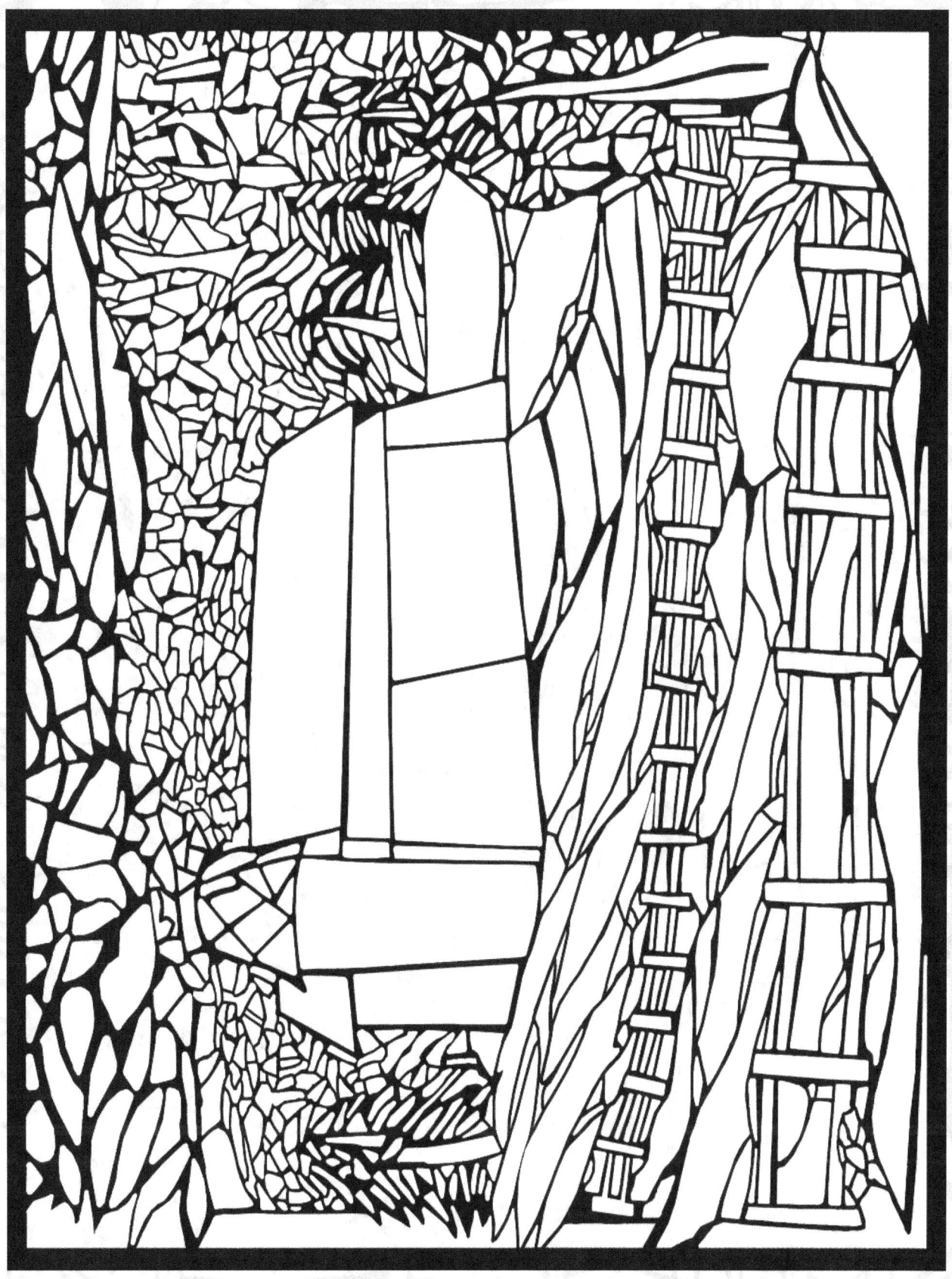

We Will Cross That Covered Bridge When We Get There

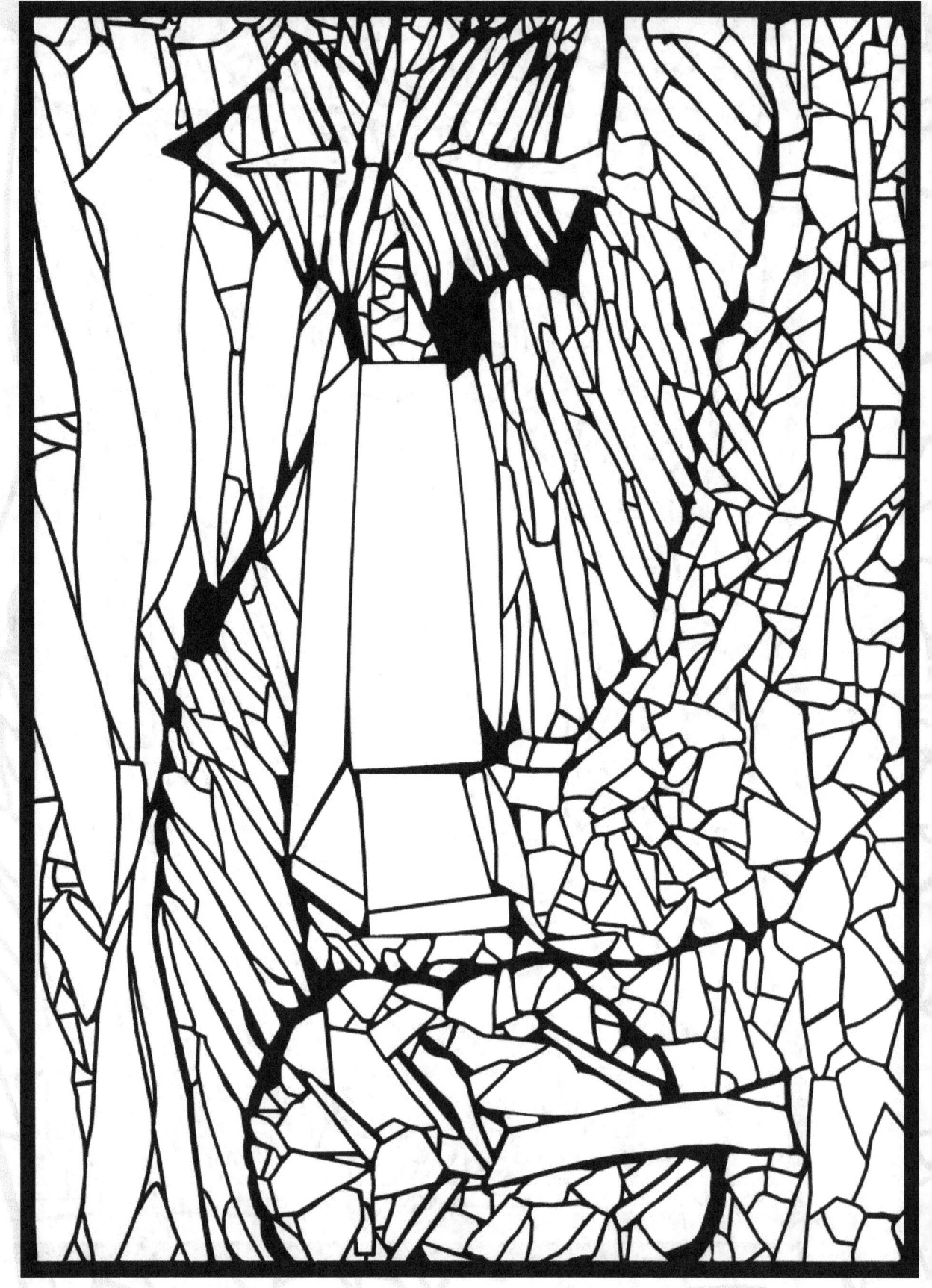

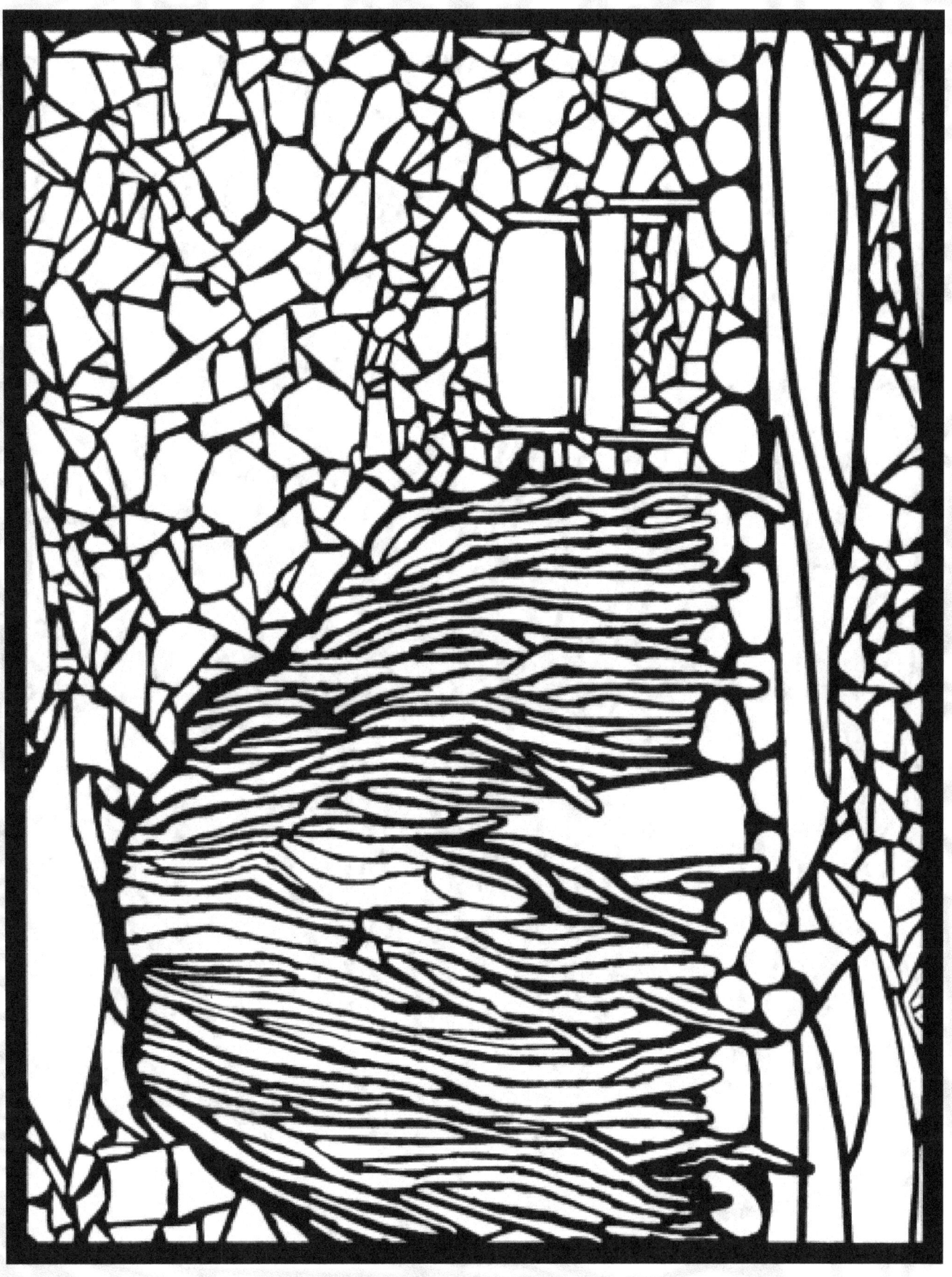

A Day at the Park

Flowers

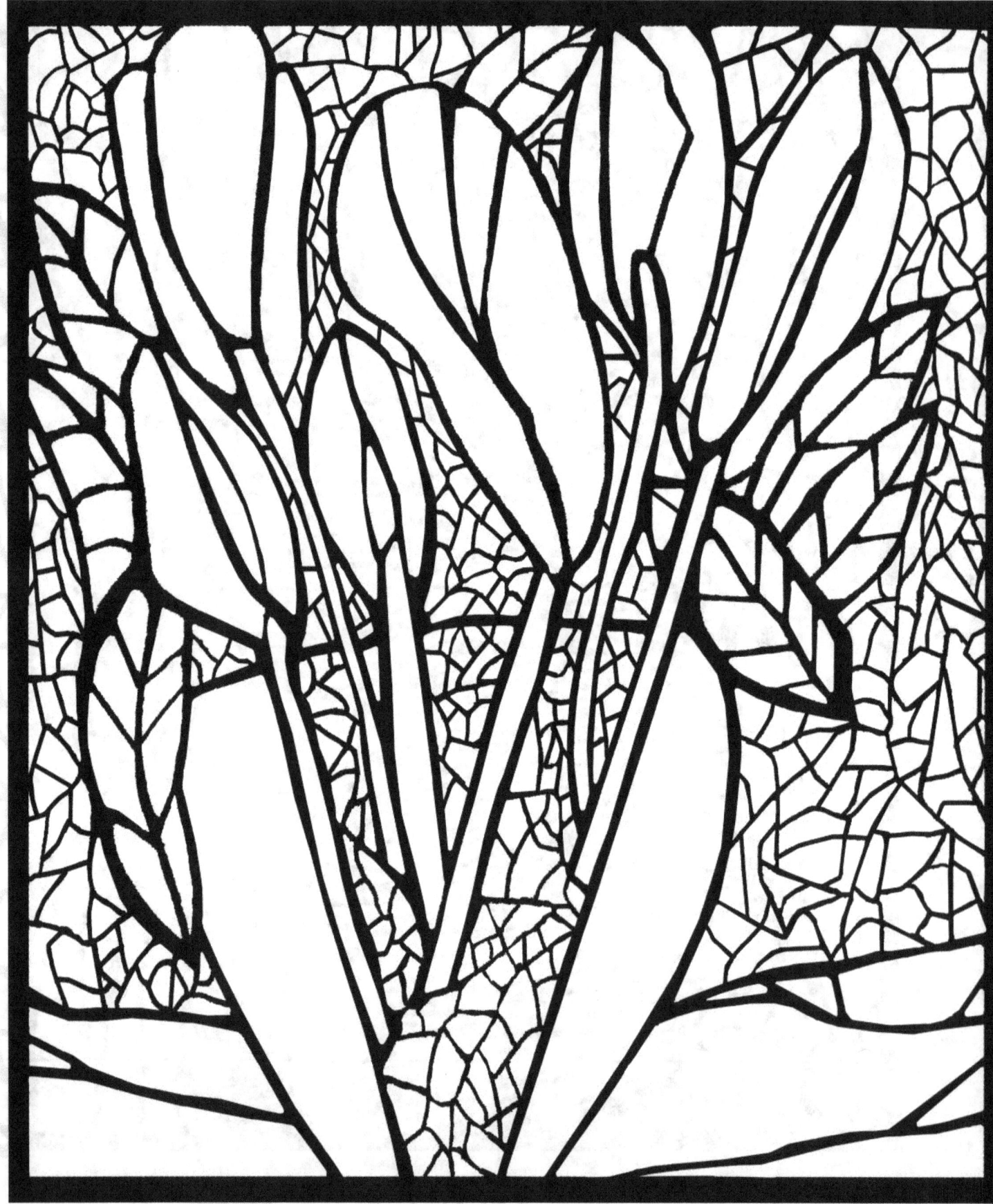

My Heart Goes To Pieces When You Are Not Near

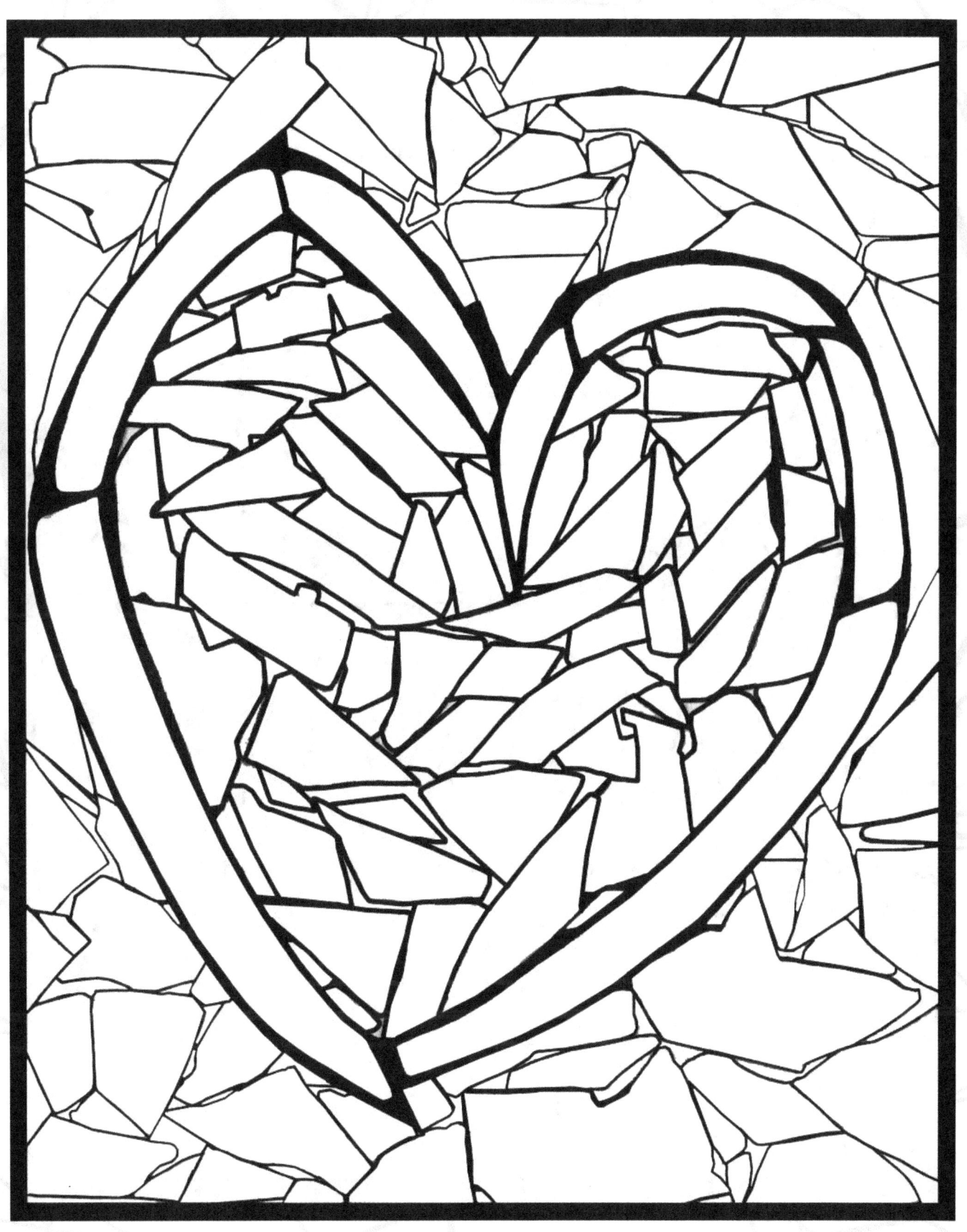

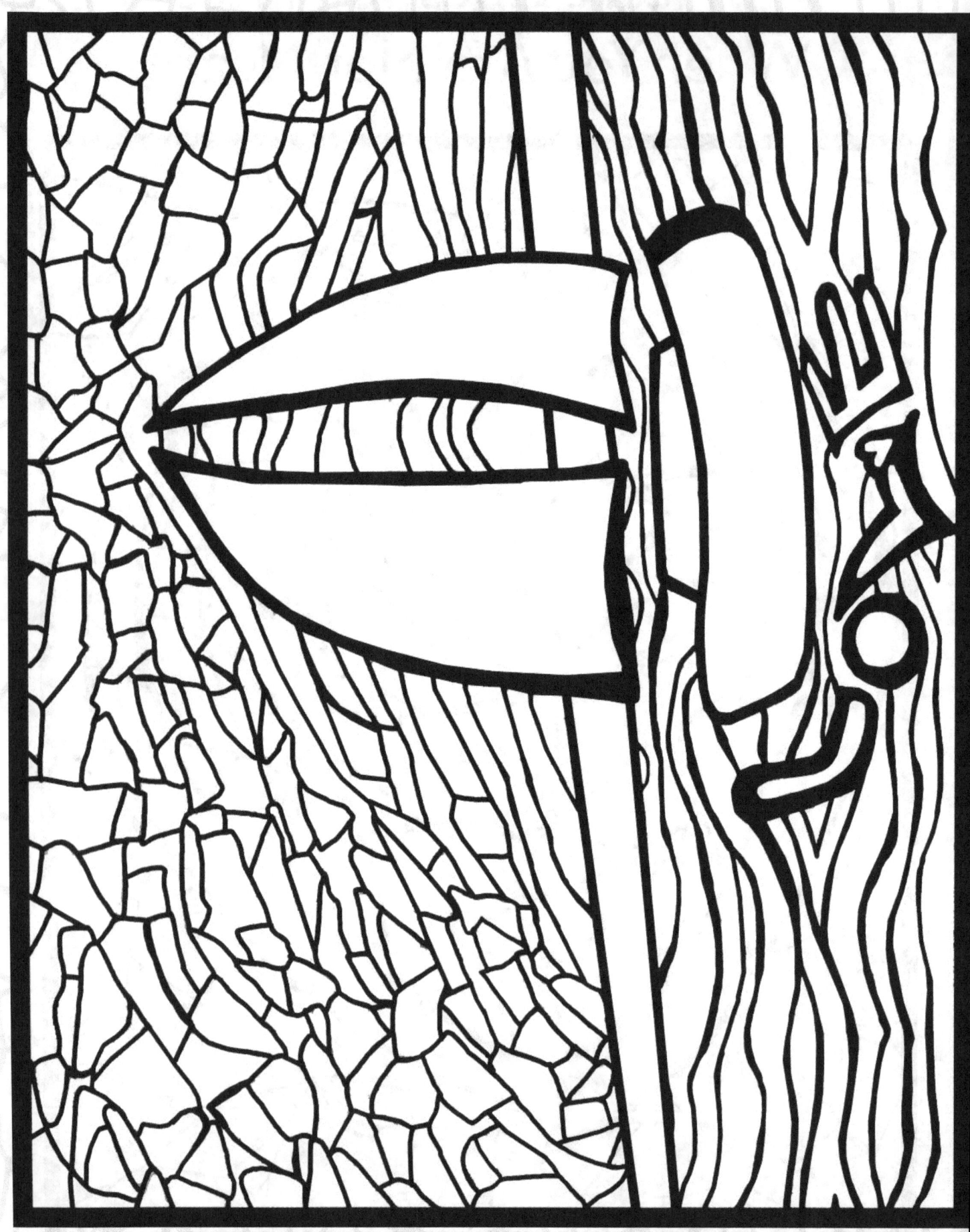

Love Will See You Through

Larry and I went to an ALS picnic where someone there told us an old parable. She said that our struggles are like a rocky or rough body of water that we can navigate by swimming or on a boat. Our "boats" are composed of our friends and families who help us get through the hard times. As we have had to deal with Larry's illness we have found this to be very true and have worked this theme into many of our mosaics. The water in this picture symbolizes our troubles - and our navigating them with the help of our friends, our family, and - you'll see the word 'love' in the water - our love.

If Larry and I could convey one thing to anyone else facing this sort of difficulty, it is that everyone in life faces challenges. ALS was a tough diagnosis to receive but instead of focusing on the negative, we focus on what Larry can do. At the beginning of 2014, Larry stopped working as an engineer and project manager. We spent the last two years of his life striving to make each day count. We enjoyed each other's company, spent our time exploring, and turned what we saw into works of art.

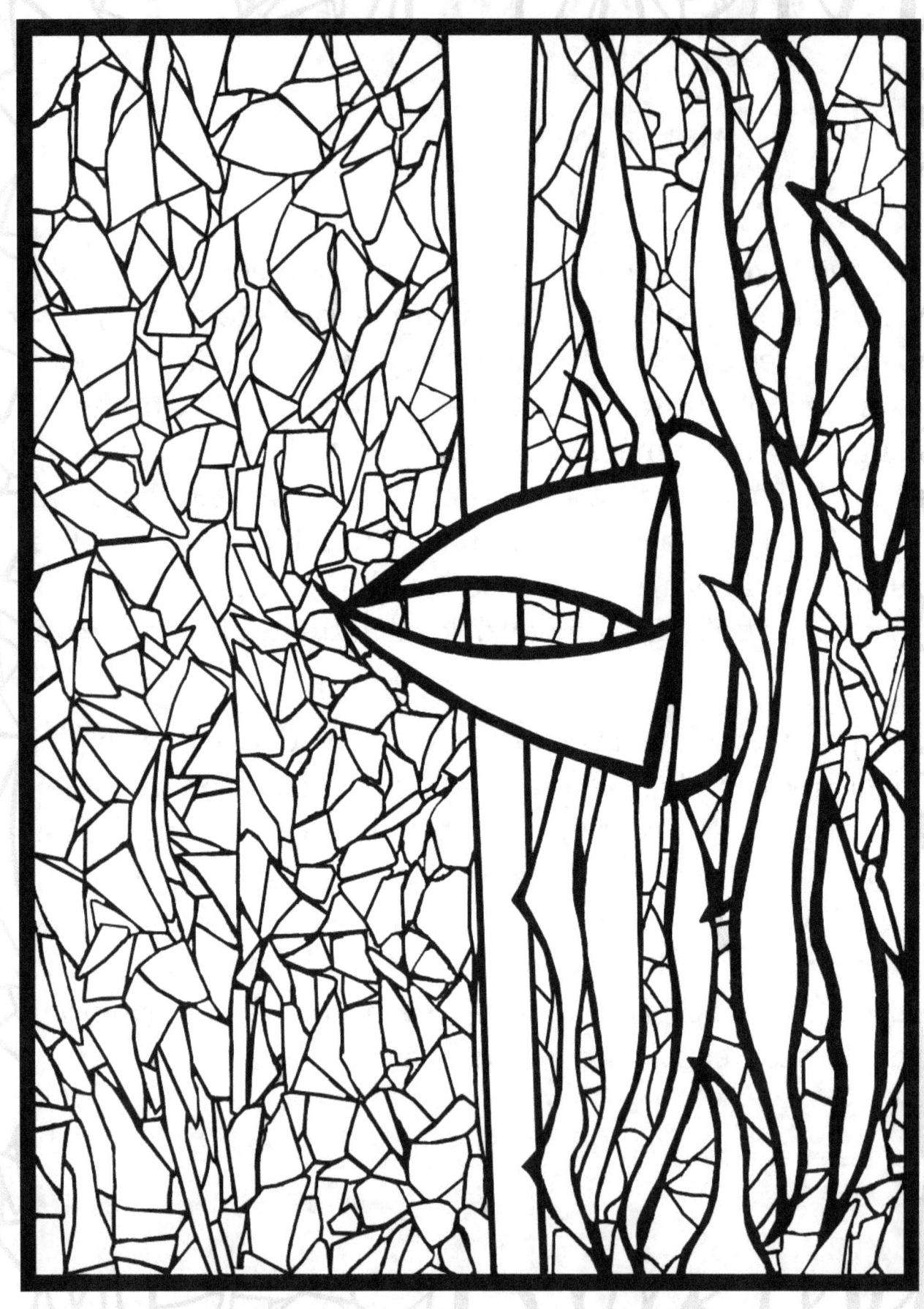

Sunset Sail On A Beautiful Summer Day

A Peaceful Butterfly

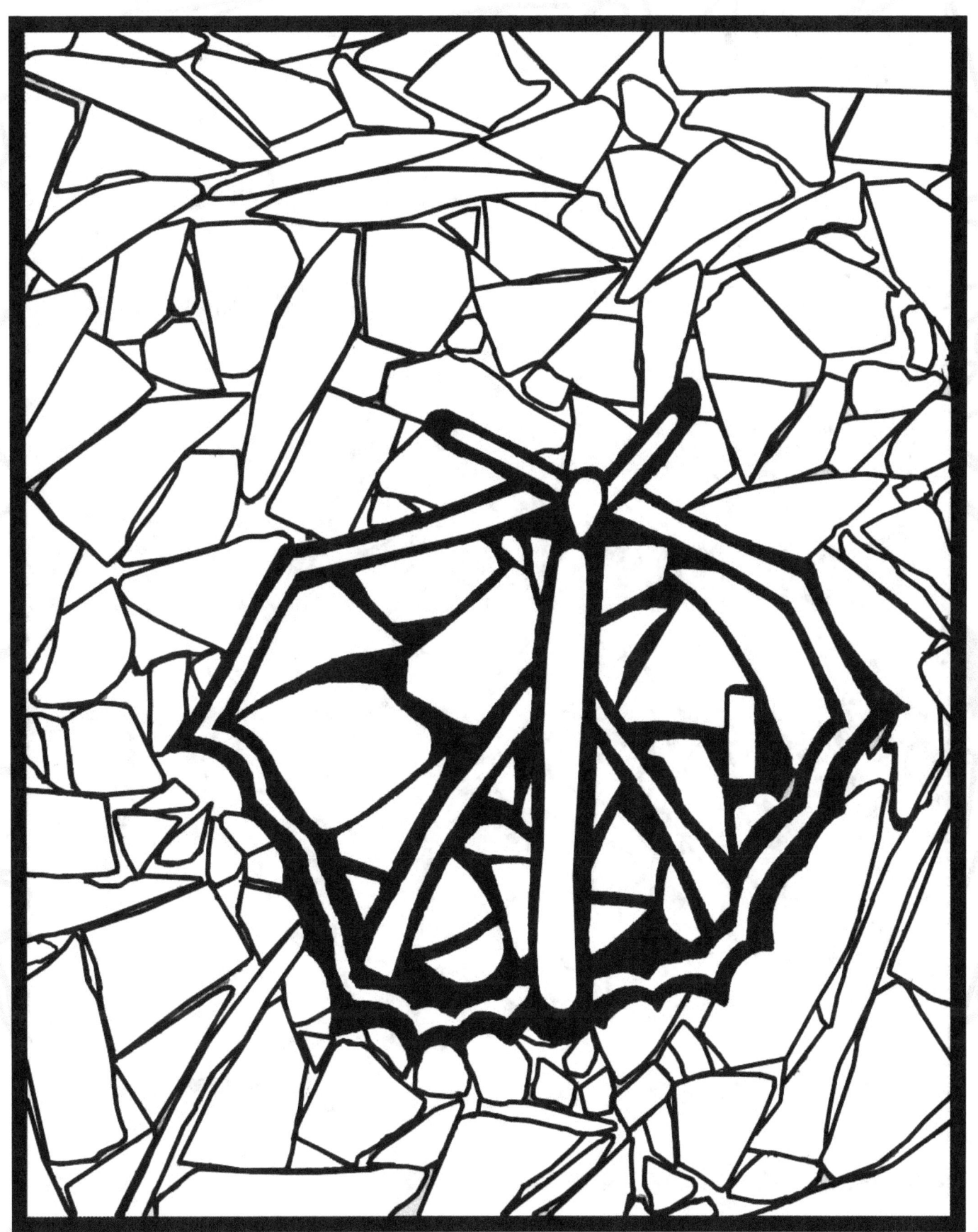

Cheers

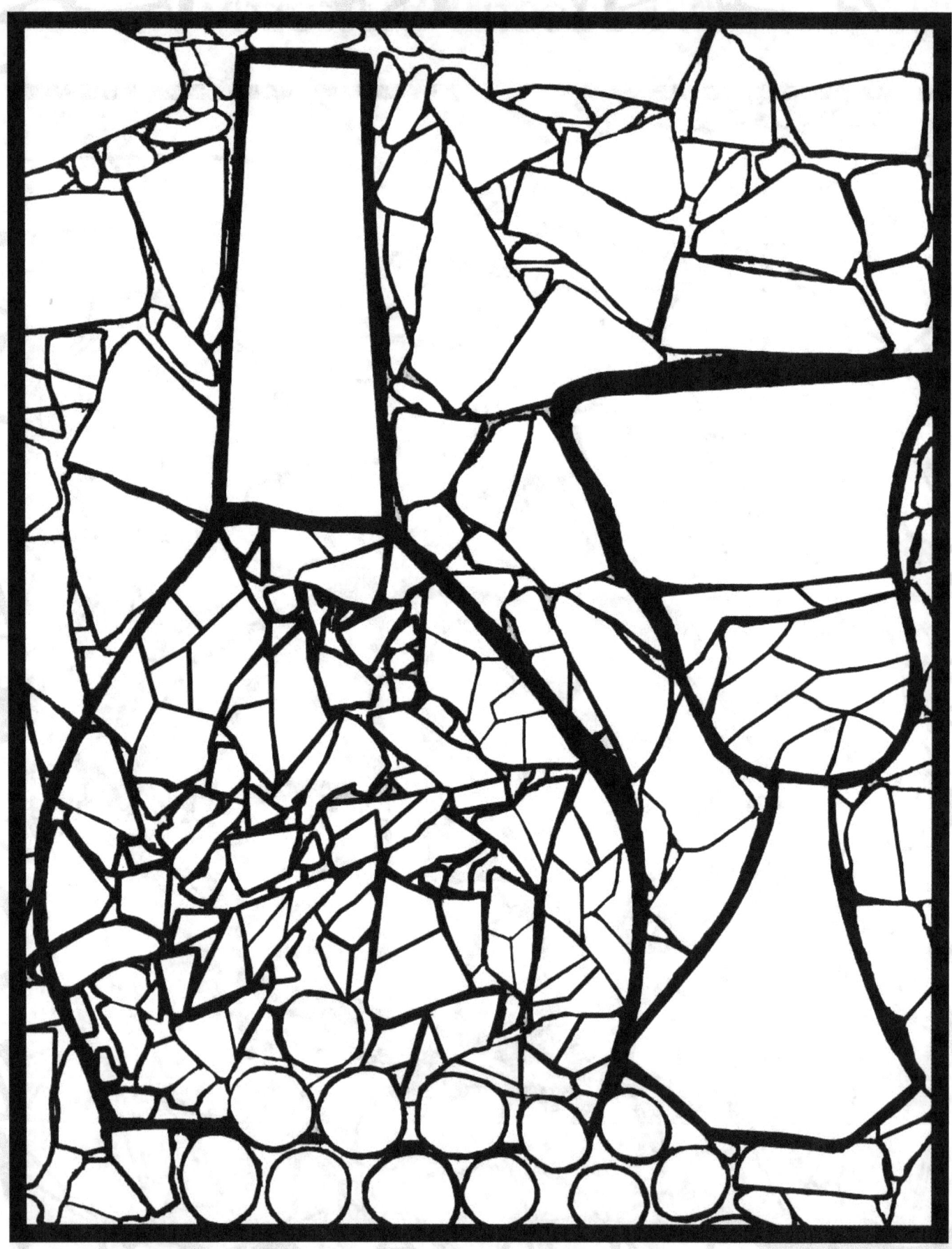

Gazebo by the Lake

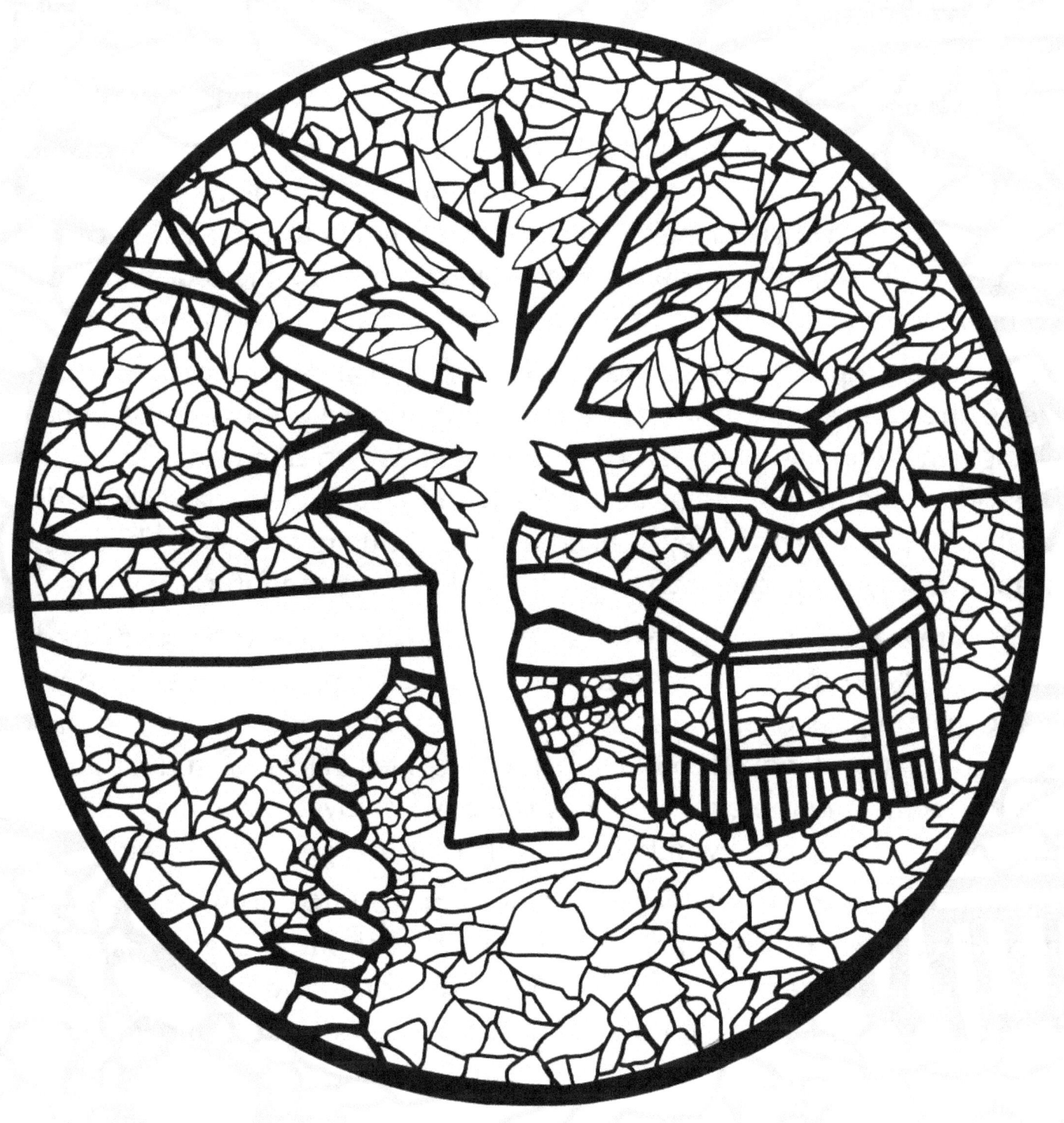

Pittsburgh

Does anyone truly appreciate the place they grew up in? The following four pictures are all about Pittsburgh.

I grew up in Pittsburgh and didn't realize what it a nice city it is until I left.

I was three when we moved to Monroeville, a suburb located east of Pittsburgh. Weekends were spent at the local mall and we didn't cross bridges or go through tunnels unless we were going to the airport or had visitors in from out of town. We would show off Pittsburgh to our company, often taking them to Mount Washington and to the incline.

Some times unpredictable events happen that changes the course of our life. Other times, we know change is coming and we prepare for it. I knew change was coming when I was 18 and went off to Simmons College in Boston. I remember standing at my dorm and watching my parents getting smaller and smaller as they walked away. I thought to myself, "the next chapter of my life is about to begin. I wonder what the future will bring?"

I was a management major with a minor in retailing. After I graduated I moved to New York City where I did an internship as an assistant buyer in a department store, Abraham and Strauss. They offered me a job and after graduation, I moved to New York where I fell in love with the theatre, the museums, and the excitement of the city. I enjoyed days off walking to the corner deli where I would buy bagels that had just been baked.

No matter where I lived, I would come back to Pittsburgh. My family is here. Pittsburghers are friendly. I could do without the gray days, but otherwise it is a great place to live. While we don't have Broadway, we do have theatre, museums, and how about Dem Stillers, Pirates, and Penguins?

I'm Inclined To Love You

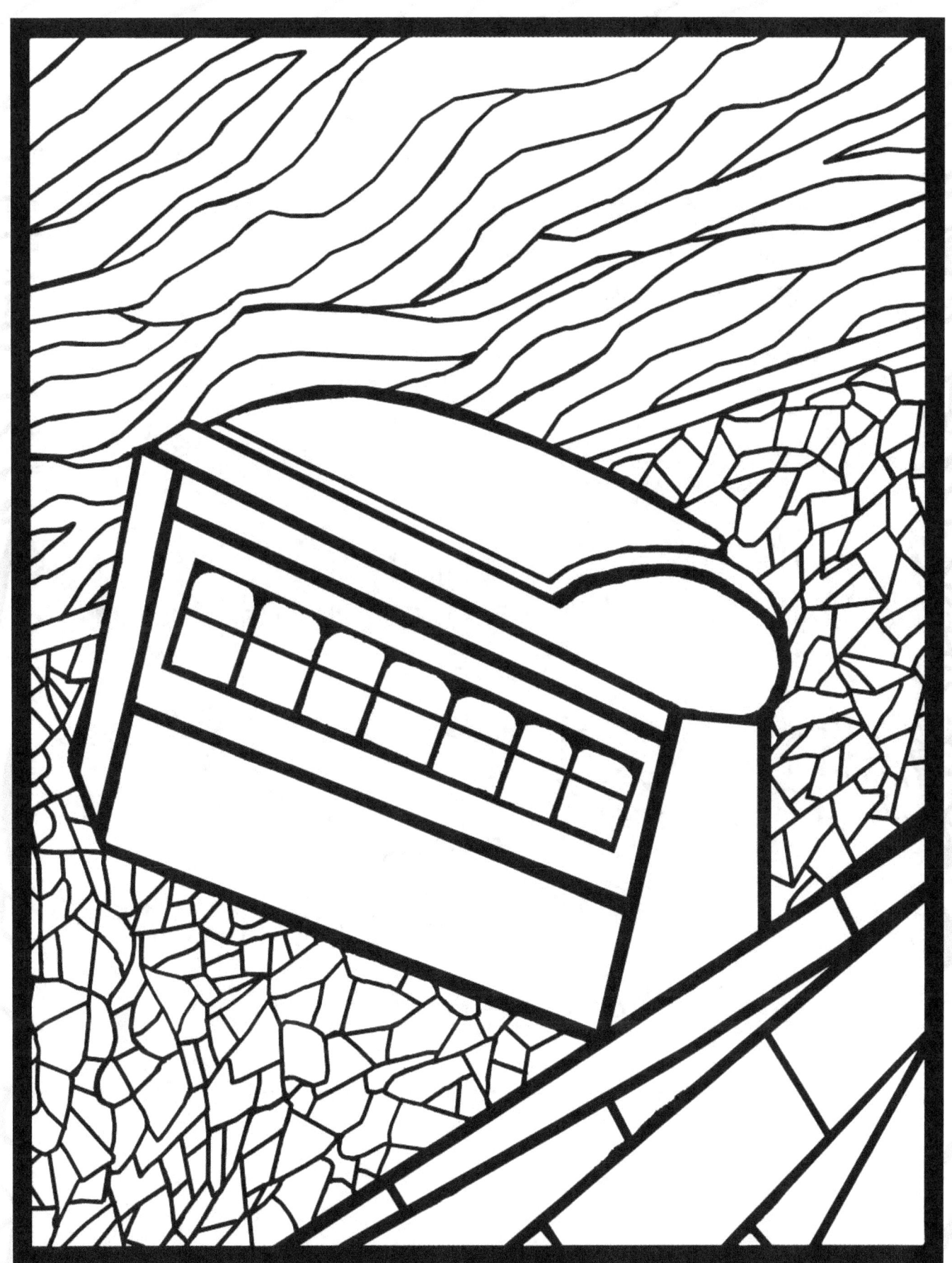

A View From The Tunnel

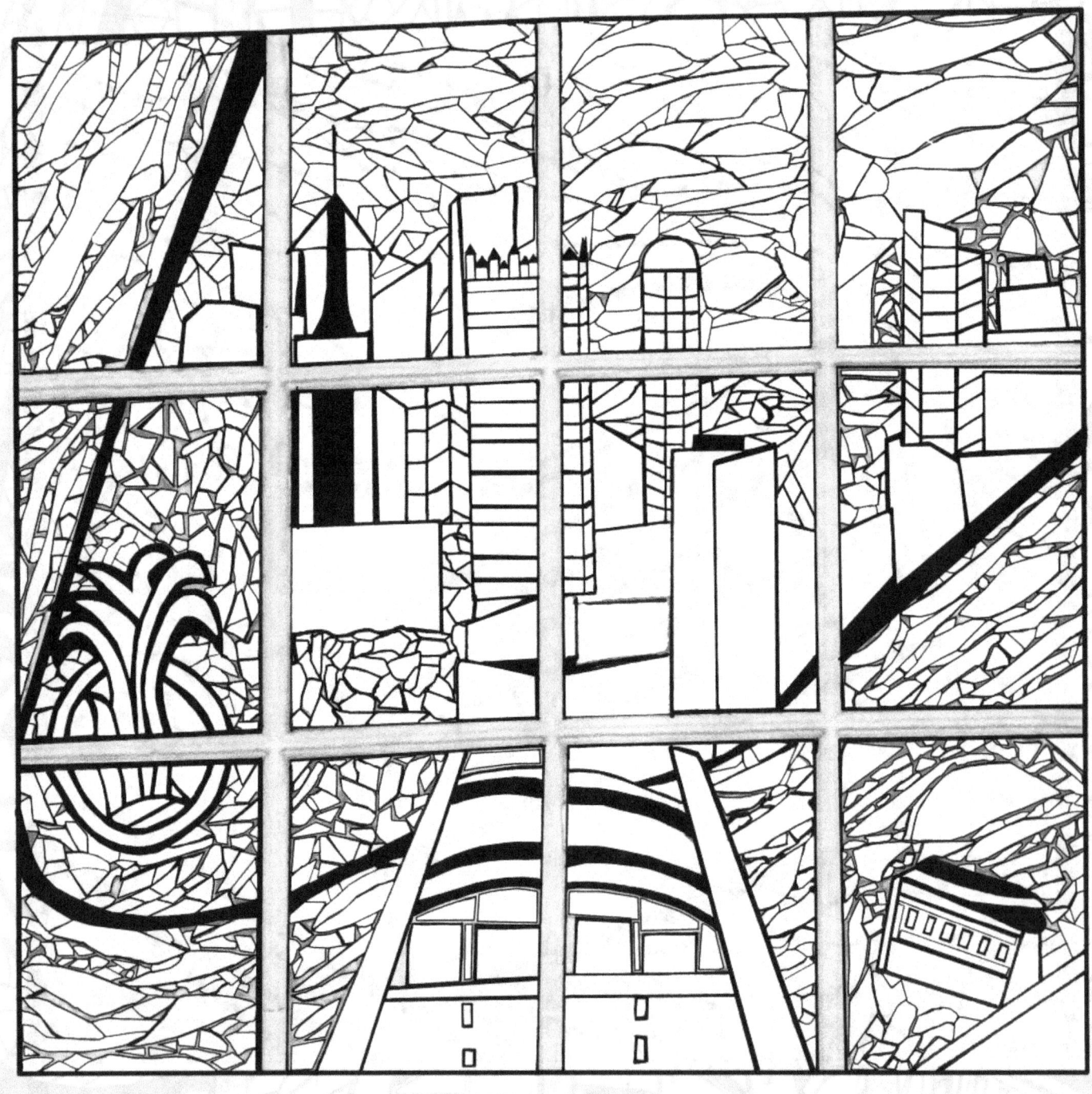

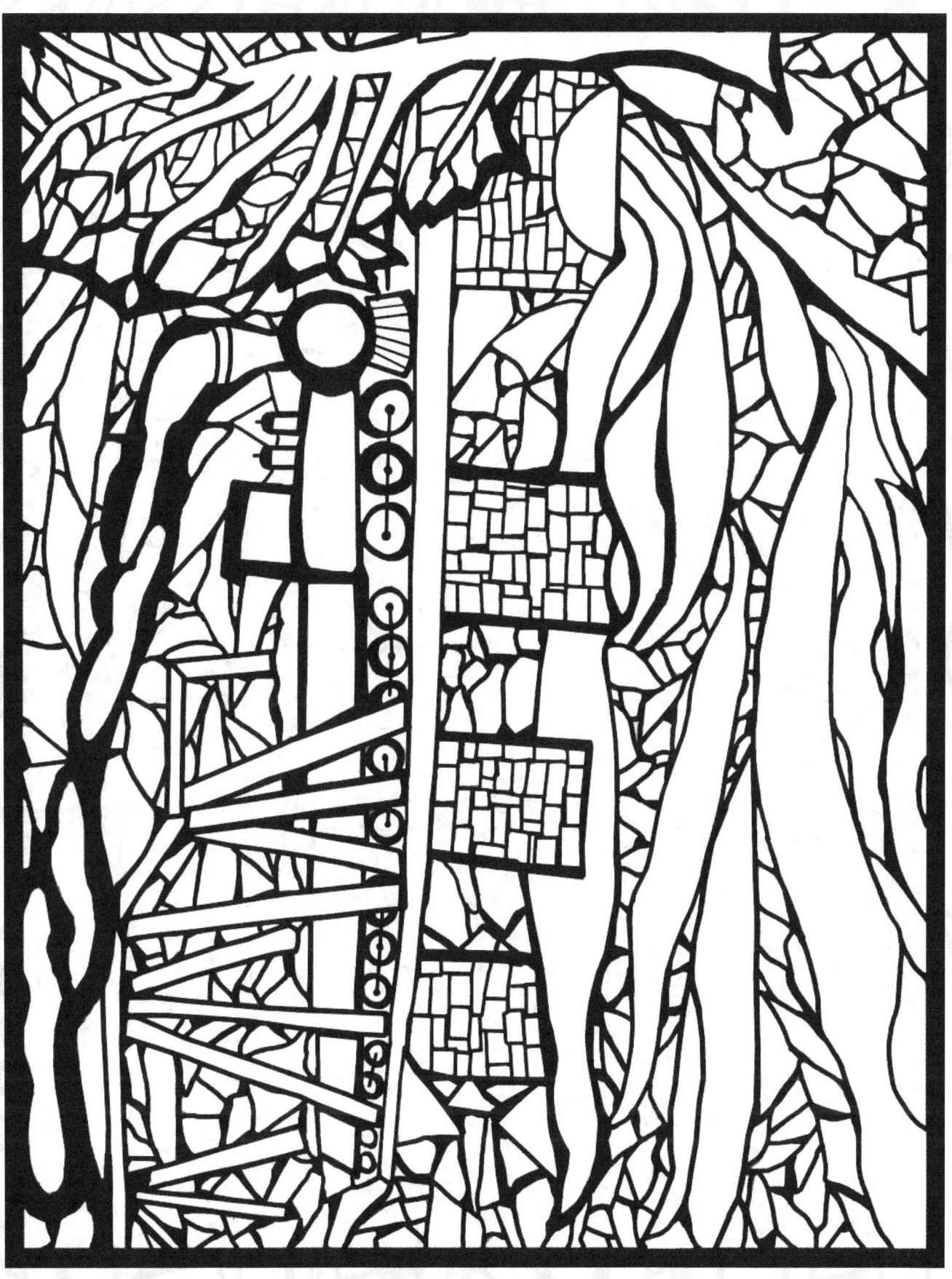

An Old Fashioned Train

Step Trek

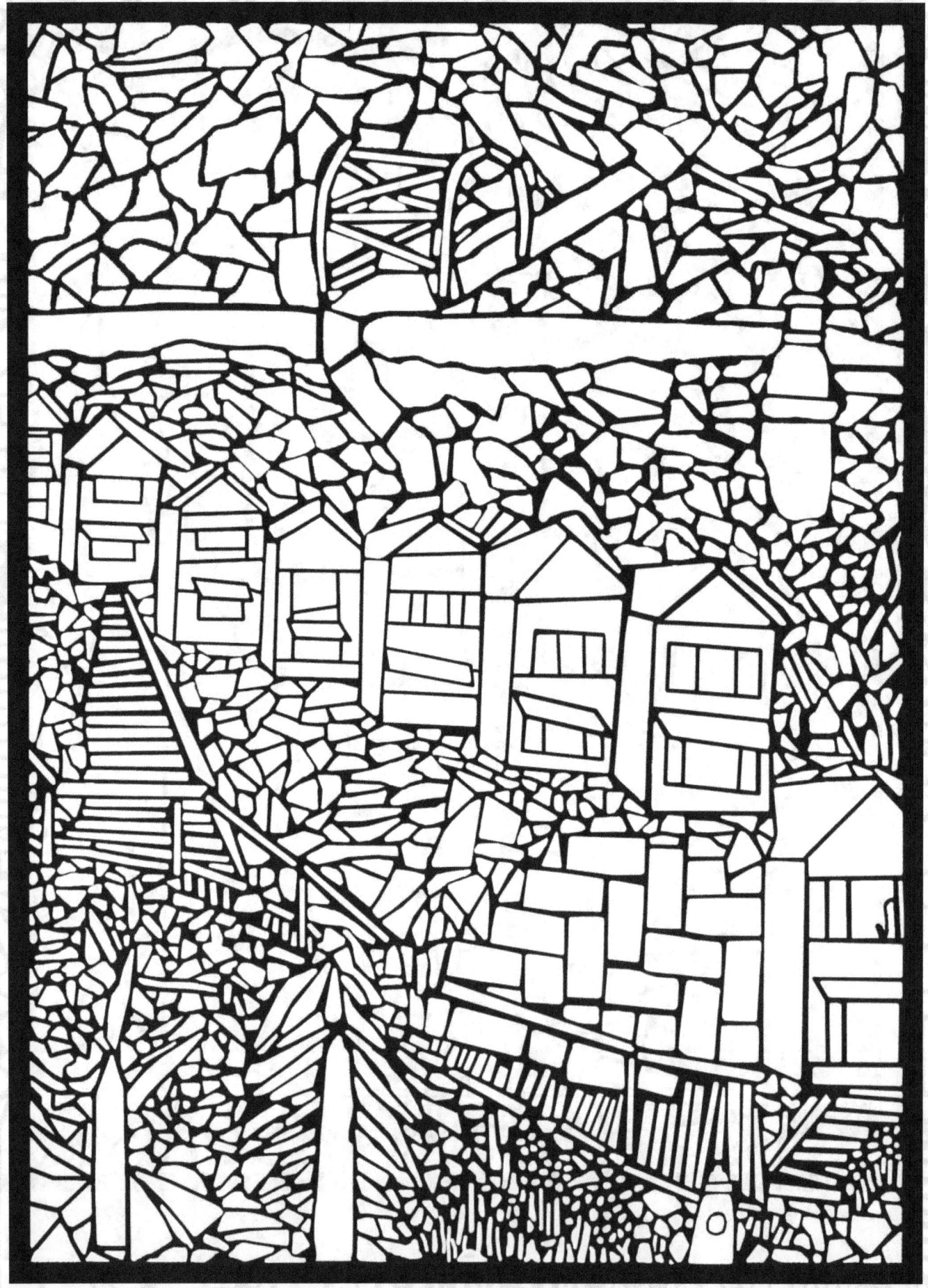

Butterflies

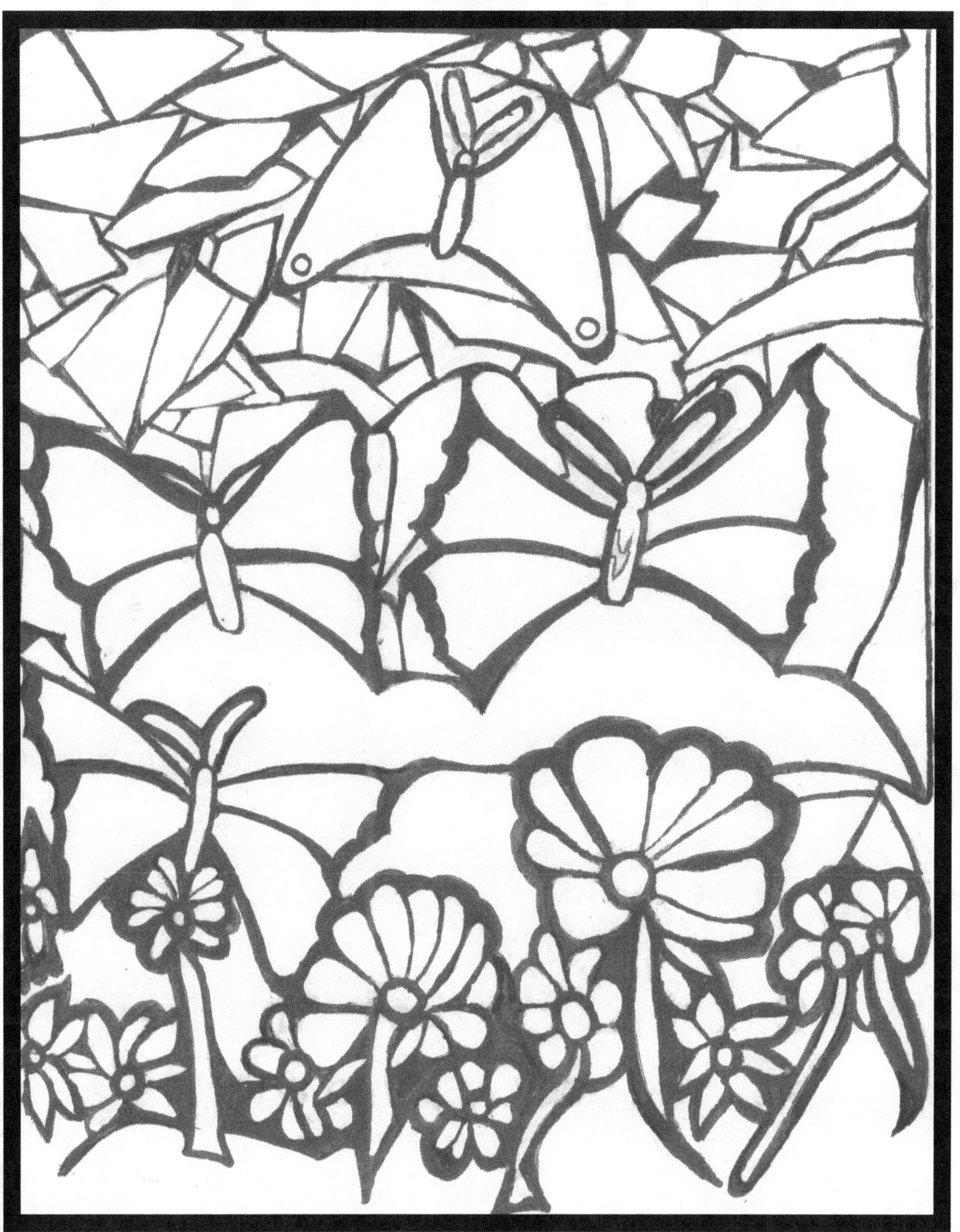

www.ingramcontent.com/pod-product-compliance
Lightning Source LLC
Chambersburg PA
CBHW081308170526
45165CB00010B/3295